The International Design Library®

MEDIEVAL FLORAL DESIGNS

by Phoebe Ann Erb

PUBLISHERS, INC.
OWINGS MILLS, MARYLAND

Introduction

THE PERIOD OF WESTERN HISTORY referred to as medieval or the Middle Ages, connecting ancient and modern times, stretched roughly a thousand years, from the disintegration of the Roman Empire in the West in the 400s until the advent of the Renaissance in the 1400s. This book features floral and figure motifs culled from textiles, manuscripts and objects of these unsettled yet richly creative and diverse years.

As the Roman Empire collapsed, barbarian invasions from the north and east caused pandemonium in Western Europe. In spite of the preoccupation with simply surviving, a few monasteries did produce manuscripts, metalwork and sculpture decorated with complex interlacing lines, spirals and circles culminating in the Celtic Book of Kells.

The stability of Charlemagne's reign (768-814) spawned a renaissance of arts in Europe. Workshops sprang up everywhere, nearly all of them attached to monasteries, which were the repositories of classical culture and learning. Monastic artists and craftsworkers excelled in blending classical and Byzantine forms, and created a new style in which figures were frequently placed within a frame of tall columns, rounded arches and decorative floral details. Artisans produced mosaics, embroideries, sculpture, metalwork, wood and ivory carvings and illuminated manuscripts.

European civilization fell into the chaos of the Dark Ages after Charlemagne's death, as his heirs, overcome by constant Viking raids, failed to maintain order and personal safety. In the tenth century, with the cessation of the raids and the foundation of the monastery of Cluny in France, peace and monastic reforms encouraged a rebirth of the arts. In England, Dunstan, a monk who became Archbishop of Canterbury, was also an artist, closely observing nature and often painting images from it. Prevailing ascetic attitudes changed to love and enjoyment of the natural world, and medieval decoration is replete with plants, flowers, birds and insects familiar to the cloister, orchard and forest. Artists, both monastic and secular, captured the flowering world while fulfilling a steady demand by the church for manuscripts, embroideries, tapestries and other objects of beauty to ignite piety and glorify God.

The impetus to spread the Christian story inspired exquisitely decorated copies of the Bible. Long hours were given to the art of illumination, and the resulting pictorial accounts of the life of Christ, framed in decorative floral arabesques or sprays of garden perennials, were one of the great creative achievements of the time. In addition to spreading biblical stories, illuminated manuscripts served to disseminate artistic styles and motifs. Since these small psalters, gospels, missals, breviaries and books of hours were easy to carry from place to place, they influenced other fields of decoration, such as mural, icon and ceramic painting, as well as relief sculpture, stained glass and embroidery.

The crusades to the Holy Land, zealously begun at the close of the eleventh century and stubbornly continued for the next 200 years, stimulated fundamental changes in European society. Towns grew; tradespeople, bankers, artisan guilds and craft unions prospered. The feudal economy, based on land, declined as money and trade expanded.

Trade with the East also spurred creative activity. From the Byzantine and Moslem worlds came thousands of novel concepts and art forms: richly embroidered banners and costumes, colorful silk textiles with rosettes, florets, palmettes, acanthus leaves and stylized animals inside medallions, cloissoné and glass.

Now, in addition to the clergy and nobility, rich merchants and traders also became patrons of the arts, commissioning jewelry, tapestries, small paintings and illuminated manuscripts for their private households.

Towns, as they grew into cities, vied with one another to build the most glorious cathedrals. Building reached a feverish pitch in the twelfth and thirteenth centuries, and this architectural explosion fostered all of the deocrative arts. The Gothic Age was in full flower.

Even as society became more stable and things were better than ever before, life remained filled with hardships. The masses strruggled for subsistence in their short lives, amid recurrent famines, devastating epidemics, local wars, widespread ignorance and superstition.

Art and design, however, belie these harsh realities throughout the Middle Ages. Instead, they convey a sense of joy and optimism in being alive. People of the day loved lively colors. Interiors of churches, stained glass windows, statues, façades of buildings, tapestries and embroidered hangings were all resplendent in brilliant colors. Gaudy banners and costumes brightened public parades and festivities. Art, rather than existing as an end in itself, served to mirror and reflect the glory of creation and of God.

Scenes, often framed and embellished with floral designs, celebrated the importance and pleasure of ordinary happenings. The margins of manuscripts are sprinkled with vignettes of daily life, frequently irrelevant to the text—cakesellers, lords going hawking, a man restraining his dog from attacking squirrels, reapers with scythes, musicians, a duck carried off by a fox, a woman churnng, knights tilting, an abbess spinning, St. Dunstan painting a butterfly, a monk and nun together in stocks and fools juggling, to list but a few.

Tapestries, woven in the medieval style, depicted the enclosed garden, the epitome of gracious living, and celebrated the repose and all the sweet pleasures found there: reading, picnicking, game-playing, conversation, music-making and needle-working. Unicorns, bubbling fountains and expeditions of knights and ladies on pleasure hunts in the woods and valleys became frequent subjects in tapestry design. Such scenes, often taken from literature, were set in a background powdered with a thousand flowers, a style still known as *mille-fleurs*.

Gothic joyfulness, alas, faded into terror as half the population perished from the Black Death in the second half of the fourteenth century. By the end of the century, however, a fresh exuberance was again in the air, as a new interest in human reason, science and mathematics emerged. The age of exploration and discovery, the Renaissance, was getting under way.

Looking back to to those earlier times, however, we marvel at the medieval ancestors of our culture, who lived through difficulties we can hardly imagine, and yet created such diverse beauty. We are awe-struck before a miniature book of hours, humbled before Chartres Cathedral and delighted by the flowers blooming all at once in tapestry fields forever.

P.A.E.

Selected Bibliography

This work would not have been possible without the Newton Free Library and the Brookline Public Library of Massachusetts. I am especially grateful to the reference librarians who fulfilled innumerable requests for books through interlibrary loans. For those who wish to read further about the Middle Ages, this selected list of titles is a good place to begin.

Backhouse, Janet. *The Bedford Book of Hours.* New York: New Amsterdam Books, 1991

Backhouse, Janet. *Books of Hours.* London: The British Library, 1985

Backhouse, Janet. *Lutrell Psalter.* New York: New Amsterdam Books, 1990

Batterberry, Michael. *Art of the Middle Ages.* New York: McGraw-Hill Book Co., 1972

Bishop, Morris. *The Horizon Book of the Middle Ages.* New York: American Heritage Publishing Co., 1968

Brown, Sarah. *Medieval Craftsmen, Glass-Painters.* Toronto: University of Toronto Press, 1991

Cherry, John. *Medieval Craftsmen, Goldsmiths.* Toronto: University of Toronto Press, 1992

Egbert, Virginia Wylie. *The Medieval Artists at Work.* Princeton: Princeton University Press, 1967

Evans, Joan. *The Flowering of the Middle Ages.* New York: Bonanza Book, 1985.

Freeman, Margaret B. *The Unicorn Tapestries.* New York: Metropolitan Museum of Art, distributed by Dutton, 1976

Fremantle, Anne. *Age of Faith.* New York: Time-Life Books, 1965

Getty, (J. Paul) Museum. *Masterpieces of the J. Paul Getty Museum, Illuminated Manuscripts.* Los Angeles: J. Paul Getty Museum, 1997

Hollander, Hans. *Early Medieval Art.* New York: Universe Books, 1974

Icher, Francois. *Building the Great Cathedrals.* New York: Harry Abrams, Inc, 1998

Jones, Mary Eirwen. *A History of Western Embroidery.* New York: Watson-Guptill Publications, 1969

McLanathan, Richard. *Pageant of Medieval Art and Life.* Philadelphia: Westminster Press, 1965

Metzger, Therese and Mendel. *Jewish Life in the Middle Ages : Illuminated Manuscripts of the 13th-16th Century.* New York: Alpine Fine Arts Collection, 1982

Millars, Meiss, Longon, Jean. *Les Tres Riches Heures: The Medieval Seasons.* New York: George Braziller, 1995

O'Neill, John, P. *Enamels of Limoges 1100-1350 .* New York: Metropolitan Museum of Art, distributed by Harry N. Abrams, 1996

Ratti, Oscar and Westbrook Adele. *The Medieval Health Handbook.* New York: George Braziller, Inc, 1976

Staniland, Kay. *Medieval Craftsmen: Embroiderers.* Toronto: University of Toronto Press, 1991

Time-Life Editors. *What Life Was Like in the Age of Chivalry.* Alexandria, VA: Time-Life Books, 1997

Weinstein, Krystyna. *The Art of Medieval Manuscripts.* San Diego: Laurel Glen Publishing, 1997

Wieck, Roger S. *Painted Prayers: The Books of Hours in Medieval and Renaissance Art.* New York: George Braziller, Inc. (in association with Pierpont Morgan Library), 1997

Wilson, David. *The Bayeaux Tapestry.* New York: Alfred A. Knopf, 1985

Yapp, W. B. *Birds in Medieval Manuscripts.* London: British Library, 1981

ILLUSTRATIONS

The drawings on the following pages are details taken from textiles, illuminated manuscripts, mosaics, enamels, paintings, stained glass and architectural ornaments. Most of the motifs have been enlarged or reduced for the purposes of this book. Identification includes, when known to the author, type of source, name and origin as well as the century in which it was made.

Lower: Manuscript. Flemish, 14th century
25 Top left: Brocade. Italian, 13th century
Lower left: Bas relief: Viviers Cathedral. French, 8th century
Right: Brocade. Italian, 13th century
26 Top and Left: Tapestry: " Lady with the Unicorn." French, 16th century
Lower right: Manuscript. Italian, 15th century
27 Top: *Book of Hours of Etienne Chevalier*. French, 15th century
Lower: Tapestry: "Lady with the Unicorn." French, 16th century
28 Top left: Manuscript. French, 15th century
Top right: Manuscript. English, 12th century
Center: Manuscript. English, 15th century
Lower: Embroidery. Sicilian, 12th century
29 Tapestry: "Lady with the Unicorn." French, 15th century
30 Top left: Stained glass. German, 12th century
Top right: Mosaic: Basilica San Marco. Venetian, 11th-13th centuries
Center: Manuscript: *Die Minnesinger*. German, 14th century
Lower: Manuscript. German, 11th century
31 Top: Panel painting. German, 15th century
Lower right: Tapestry: "Angers Apocalypse." French, 15th century
Lower left: Manuscript. French, 15th century
32 Tapestry. French, 15th century
33 Top: Embroidered altar cloth. German, 14th century
Lower: Manuscript: *Godescalc*. Carolingian, 8th century
34 Left: Book of Hours. English, 14th century
Right: Embroidery. German, 14th century
35 Top left: Book of Hours. English, 14th century
Top right: *Lutrell Psalter*. English, 14th century
Lower: Tapestry. Flemish, 14th century
36 Top: Manuscript. German, 14th century
Left: Mosaic: Church of Sordes. French, 11th century
Top right: Textile from painting. Franco-Flemish, 15th century
Center right: Manuscript. English, 14th century
Lower: Manuscript, *Breviary du John duc de Burgandy*. French, 15th century
37 Top: Wall decoration: Sainte Chapelle. French, 13th century
Lower: Mosaic: Basilica San Marco. Venetian, 11th-13th century
38 Top left: Playing cards. French, 13th century
Top right: Heraldic design. English, 14th century
Lower left: Book of Hours. French, 15th century
Lower right: Manuscript. French, 15th century
39 Top: Mosaic: Basilica St. Vitale. Italian, 6th century
Lower: Manuscript. Armenian, 12th century
40 Top: Wall decoration: Sainte Chapelle. French, 13th century

Lower left: Textile from painting. Spanish, 15th century
Lower right: Embroidered textile. French, 14th century
41 Brocade. Venetian, 15th century
42 Top: Brocade. Italian, 13th century
Center: Textile from painting. Czech, 14th century
Lower: Brocade. Italian, 14th century

13

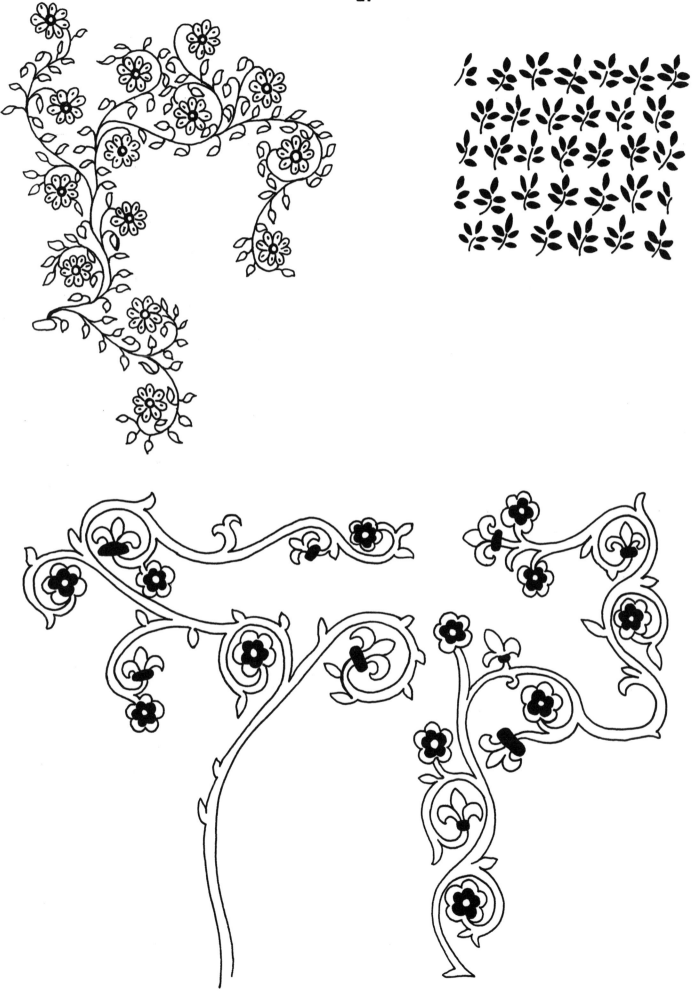

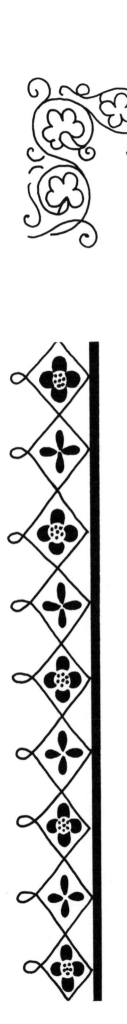